In the Stillness of the Mind:

Always remember:

You are not the Dancer
— You are the Dance!

Jay Joyful

SAMADHI

A Musical Journey to Peace, Connection, and Joy

A CONTEMPLATIVE SONGBOOK

Joyful-Life.org

Publisher: BoD · Books on Demand GmbH, Überseering 33, 22297 Hamburg, bod@bod.de
Print: Libri Plureos GmbH, Friedensallee 273, 22763 Hamburg
ISBN: **978-3-8192-2994-7**

Content

The Songs

Appendix

Jay Joyful

Jay Joyful is an artist on a soulful mission to uplift the world through the universal language of music. Rooted in reggae rhythms and inspired by themes of unity, harmony, and inner Peace, Jay's music invites listeners to embark on a journey of self-discovery and collective empowerment. His songs reflect a deep Love for humanity and the planet, blending poetic lyrics with soothing melodies that resonate with the heart and soul.

Jay Joyful's sound is more than just music – it's a message. His work explores themes of Love, personal growth, and the search for meaning, with a particular focus on finding Peace amid Life's challenges. Whether it's through groovy reggae beats or introspective acoustic rhythms, Jay's artistry aims to inspire people to embrace their authentic selves and spread positivity to others.

His debut album, "*Mambo Poa* – Surfin' on the Waves of Life", captures his philosophy of riding Life's ups and downs with grace, humour, and joy. – Now, in his second reggae album, "Samadhi", he weaves again together playful rhythms with spiritual insights, offering both entertainment and contemplation.

Jay Joyful's music is a celebration of Life's interconnectedness, echoing his core belief that Love is the greatest power, Peace is the ultimate goal, and Joy is the energy that binds them all. In every beat and lyric,

Jay invites the listener to join him on a journey toward a more mindful world, with open hearts and joyful minds.

Tanzania, May 2025

Lusungu Nkwera

Listen to Jay Joyful's music, e.g. on Spotify:

also on:

Apple Music, iTunes, Instagram/Facebook, TikTok and other ByteDance stores, YouTube Music, Amazon, Pandora, Deezer, Tidal, iHeartRadio, Claro Música, Saavn, Boomplay, Anghami, NetEase, Tencent, Qobuz, Joox, Kuack Media, Adaptr, Flo, MediaNet

About the Album

Step into a world where melodies meet mindfulness and rhythms echo the heartbeat of nature. *"Samadhi"* is a vibrant reggae album that weaves together soulful storytelling, uplifting anthems, and meditative soundscapes. Each track invites you to explore the harmony between the elements, the cycles of Life, and the essence of freedom.

"Samadhi" takes its name from a Sanskrit word that signifies a state of profound meditation, spiritual enlightenment, and ultimate unity with the cosmos. This reggae album is more than just a collection of songs – it is a journey through the interconnectedness of Life, the rhythm of the Earth, and the search for inner harmony. Each track carries its own unique energy, guiding listeners through a transformative experience that mirrors the essence of *Samadhi*.

The title track, *"Samadhi"*, serves as the spiritual heart of the album, embodying the quest for balance and transcendence. Songs like *"The Wave and the Ocean"* delve into metaphors of unity, reflecting on the eternal dance between individuality and the collective whole.

"Doctor Forest" celebrates the healing power of nature, reminding us of our sacred bond with the Earth. In contrast, tracks like "Beachparty" and *"Pili-pili"* burst with energy, inspiring liberation, joy, and vibrant self-expression.

The playful, yet inspiring, "The Monkey's Song" and soulful "Donkey's Song" add moments of whimsy and depth, creating a rich tapestry of moods and themes.

The album also explores Life's spiritual and moral cycles, as captured in "Freedom" and "Karma Comes Back".

And as the journey winds through the joyful beats, it leaves listeners with a sense of celebration, grounding them in the simple, blissful pleasures of Life.

The album ends with *"Amani"*, a tranquil instrumental piece that reflects with serene and meditative tones, inviting listeners to slow down and connect deeply.

"Samadhi" isn't just music; it's a journey: Through its melodies, rhythms, and lyrics, Samadhi invites you to dance between the spiritual and the earthly, the introspective and the exuberant. It is a call to embrace Life's infinite beauty, to find unity within and without, and to carry the Peace of Samadhi into every moment of your journey. Perfect for reggae lovers, spiritual seekers, and anyone who wishes to feel the rhythm of Life resonate in their soul.

The Silent Dancer's Guide

A Companion for your Journey toward Samadhi

When you're dancing the path of stillness and awakening, here are some gentle reminders to keep close to your heart:

🌸 1. Be Here – Be Now

Samadhi begins where the mind ends. Let go of past and future – they are but shadows. Rest in the eternal Now. Feel the breath. Hear the silence. This is where the Divine dwells.

💧 2. Surrender the Self

You are not the doer. You are the space in which all happens. Don't try to reach Samadhi – allow it to arrive when the ego softens and all striving fades.

🔥 3. Let the Inner Flame Guide You

Within you is a quiet fire – awareness itself. Stay close to it. This flame does not burn; it illumines. When thoughts come, return to the flame. When doubts arise, let the light lead the way.

🌸 4. Embrace Everything, Resist Nothing

Silence does not mean avoidance. In Samadhi, all is embraced – joy and sorrow, light and shadow. Let your consciousness hold everything like the sky holds the clouds – untouched, yet present.

🪶 5. Move like Wind, Rest like Earth

In this dance of Life, move with grace, but be grounded. Flow through experiences, but let your roots sink into stillness. Samadhi is the art of *moving deeply within even as Life unfolds outside.*

🌙 6. Drop the Labels, Feel the Essence

You are not your name, your role, your belief, your story. You are the one who watches it all – formless, vast, and free. Let go of identity, and the truth will bloom like a lotus from within.

🌙 7. Be Gentle with the Mind

Do not fight your thoughts. Watch them. Smile at them. Let them pass like birds across the sky. The more gently you observe, the more silence will grow. That silence is the doorway to Samadhi.

☀ 8. Trust the Pathless Path

Samadhi cannot be mapped or forced. Each step you take disappears behind you. Walk with trust. Sometimes, it feels like nothing is happening – but beneath the surface, you are dissolving.

🌱 9. Tune in to the Sacred Rhythm

Life has a pulse – listen. Every moment is a mantra, every breath a prayer. Samadhi is not elsewhere – it is right here, in the rhythm of your breath, in the stillness behind every sound.

🎵 10. Let it Become a Dance

When you let go of the need to achieve, Samadhi becomes a dance – effortless, fluid, alive. No fear, no control, no destination. Just presence, awareness, bliss. You don't walk to Samadhi – you dissolve into it.

🖼 "Samadhi is not something to find – it is what remains when all else is surrendered." 🕊

So close your eyes, open your heart, and step into the silence. –

Let every breath be your guide.

Let every moment be enough.

Titles of this Album

1. *Samadhi* (7:48) – Follow with the title track to establish the album's spiritual and central theme.

2. *The Wave and the Ocean* (5:09) – A reflective and metaphorical piece to deepen the mood.

3. *Doctor Forest* (7:28) – A grounded, nature-inspired narrative about healing.

4. *Freedom* (3:38) – A liberating and uplifting anthem with a deeper meaning.

5. *The Monkey's Song* (5:39) – Playfulness and whimsy listening to the monkeys' wisdom.

6. *Karma Comes Back* (3:18) – Reflect on Life's interconnectedness with a meaningful transition.

7. *Donkey's Song* (2:26) – Donkeys are mostly misjudged, yet they are so diligent and tenacious.

8. *Pilipili* (5.54) – Did you ever got a food so delicious, but so spicy hot at the same time?

9. *Beach Party* (3:50) – A lovers' rendezvous turning into a beach party, but celebrating the erotic vibe in the end.

10. *The Coconut Tree* (3:40) – Looking at the coconut trees remind us of own resilience.

11. *Amani (instrumental)* (2:30) – A serene and instrumental reflection to set a more meditative tone.

Scan this code to listen to the album on Youtube:

About Samadhi

In the stillness of a quiet mind, when the waves of thought settle, there emerges a space untouched by time, free of duality. This space is Samadhi – a state of profound unity where the self dissolves into the vastness of existence. What does it mean to reach such a state? How does one prepare to enter this sacred dimension of being?

Samadhi is not a destination to be reached, but a homecoming to the truth that has always been within us. It is the great unveiling, a recognition of our essence as one with all that is. In Samadhi, the boundaries that define us as separate entities – the roles, identities, and fears – melt away, leaving only pure awareness. There is no "I" or "you," no striving or seeking, only the boundless presence of being.

To contemplate Samadhi is to turn inward and listen to the silence that underlies all sound. It is to see the impermanence of the world not as a source of suffering but as a reminder of the eternal. Each breath, each moment, is an opportunity to step closer to this state of surrender and union.

The path to Samadhi is one of letting go. Letting go of attachments, expectations, and the illusions of control. It is a journey into trust, into allowing the divine flow of Life to carry us. Yet, this surrender is not passive. It requires the courage to face ourselves, to sit with discomfort, and to peel away the layers of conditioning that obscure the light within.

Samadhi invites us to see beyond opposites, beyond right and wrong, pleasure and pain, gain and loss. It is the embrace of all things as they are, free from judgment and resistance. In this embrace, we come to understand that the wave is not separate from the ocean, just as we are not separate from the universe. The wave rises and falls, but the ocean remains. So, too, does our essence remain, untouched by the comings and goings of Life.

What would it feel like to live from this place of unity? To walk through the world with the awareness that all beings, all things, are interconnected? In Samadhi, every encounter becomes a reflection of the divine. The trees, the stars, the laughter of a child – all are mirrors of the same infinite presence. To live in Samadhi is to move through Life with grace and compassion, rooted in the unshakable knowing that we are one.

Yet, Samadhi is not merely an individual experience. It is a gift to the world. When one person touches this state, it radiates outward, like ripples on a still pond. The Peace and Love that arise in Samadhi have the power to heal, to transform not only the self but the collective consciousness.

So, let us sit in stillness and open ourselves to this sacred possibility. Let us soften our grip on the small self and rest in the vastness of being. Let us remember that Samadhi is not somewhere out there to be found but here, now, waiting to be realised. In every breath, in every moment, the door is open.

Meanwhile, listen ...

The Songs

Samadhi

There are moments in Life when words become more than messages – they become medicine. The song *"Samadhi"* is one of those rare offerings: a musical invitation to surrender, to remember who we are beyond fear and striving, beyond thought and form. In the beat of reggae, in the flow of breath, it gently points toward the deepest of all human longings – the longing for unity, stillness, Peace. The longing to simply be.

This song is not just to be heard. It is to be *entered*, like a river that carries the soul home.

The Recognition of Suffering

The song begins with *eyes wide open*. It does not shy away from pain or pretend that everything is easy. It speaks directly to the human heart burdened by effort, conflict, and confusion:

> *I see you struggling, I see you sad*
>
> *I see you fighting battles,*
> *feeling trapped and mad*

There is such tenderness in these lines – not judgment, but understanding. The singer is not above the struggle. He is a companion, a witness, a mirror. This is the beginning of healing: to be seen, to be acknowledged in our rawness.

But what follows is even more profound: an invitation to let go. Not to escape, but to shift – from resistance to rhythm, from effort to flow:

> *No need to wrestle, no need to run*
>
> *Flow with the rhythm –*
> *your journey's begun*

This line opens the door. The journey is not toward something new. It's a return to what has always been – the rhythm of Life itself.

The Ocean and the Wave – The Wisdom of Non-Duality

At the heart of the song lies a timeless teaching found in the mystic traditions of East and West alike: that separation is illusion. The wave and the ocean – the part and the whole – are never truly apart:

> *I am the wave and the ocean,*
> *the dancer and the dance"*

This is not a metaphor, but a spiritual truth. We believe ourselves to be isolated drops, fragile and small. But in essence, we are expressions of the *whole ocean of being*, playing for a moment in individual form. The wave rises and falls, but the ocean remains. Our true nature is not our personality or history – it is the presence that moves through all things.

This realisation is not philosophical – it is *liberation*. It is the end of fear, the end of the desperate clinging to identity. When we know we are not separate, the whole universe becomes our family. Every moment becomes sacred.

Surrender: The Sacred Art of Letting Go

The chorus becomes a mantra of surrender, echoing again and again the gentle call to stop fighting and start flowing:

This is the essence of the song. Samadhi is not a state we achieve through force, but a natural flowering that happens when we let go. When the ego steps aside, the river takes over. When the mind stops grasping, the heart starts dancing.

In a world obsessed with control, achievement, and answers, surrender sounds like defeat. But in truth, surrender is the most powerful act of trust – to *lean into Life*, to allow the dance to unfold, to *stop trying and start being*. This surrender is not passive; it is *alive*, alert, rooted in presence.

The End of Striving, the Beginning of Stillness

The second verse reminds us of the futility of chasing fulfilment:

This is the condition of most lives – running from discomfort, chasing some imagined future, endlessly analysing and worrying. The song gently disrupts this trance:

Here is a spiritual revolution: *Stop solving. Start listening*. Life is not a problem. It is a poem, a wave, a sacred dance. When we stop trying to fix it, we begin to feel it. When we stop resisting, we are carried by it.

Breath, Presence, and the Gateway to Samadhi

In the bridge, the song becomes a meditation – a rhythmic breathing in of *presence*:

> *Breathe in Peace, exhale the fear*
> *Feel the flow that brought you here*

Each breath is a doorway. Inhale, and you receive the universe. Exhale, and you let go of everything you don't need. This is not abstract – it is *visceral*. The breath is the anchor to this moment, and *this moment* is where Samadhi lives.

> *No need to grasp, no need to hold*
> *In the stream of Life, just let it unfold*

This stream – this ever-moving, ever-loving river of being – is our true home. There is nothing to control, because everything belongs. Even pain, even confusion, even death – they are part of the rhythm. To be in Samadhi is not to escape Life. It is to *merge with Life completely*, to say yes to all of it, as it is.

Cosmic Dance, Eternal Presence

In the final verses, the song expands into cosmic vision:

> *Dance with the stars in perfect harmony*
> *There's no end, no beginning, just the*
> *great unseen*

This is where the song transcends genre and becomes scripture. The dance continues – from dusk till dawn, from Life to death, from self to selflessness. Samadhi is not a private experience. It is the universal state of being when all separation dissolves, and only Love remains.

The last line is not a conclusion. It is an *invitation*:

> *Samadhi – come dance with me.*

Not as teacher and student, not as saviour and seeker – but as companions, as waves in the same ocean, as dancers in the eternal dance.

Closing Reflections: The Song as Practice

"*Samadhi*" is not just a song to listen to – it is a practice to embody.

Each time you breathe with its rhythm, you enter the presence it points to.

Each time you let go of judgment, you step closer to Samadhi.

Each time you stop trying to control and simply flow, you are already dancing.

This song teaches without preaching. It leads without pushing. It is the sound of spiritual truth clothed in warmth, melody, and rhythm. It is the voice of a friend who remembers, calling you to remember too:

> You are the wave.
> You are the ocean.
> You are already home.

Samadhi is here. In this breath. In this beat. In this moment.

Let go. Listen. Dance. And know – you are one with all.

The Lyrics

[Verse 1]

I see you struggling, I see you sad
I see you fighting battles, feeling trapped and mad
You gave up trying to understand
Lost in the chaos, slipping through your hands

But listen now, there's a different way
Where Peace will guide you, night and day
No need to wrestle, no need to run
Flow with the rhythm – your journey's begun

[Pre-Chorus]

I am the wave and the ocean, the dancer and the dance
The wave believes it begins and ends
But there's no birth, no death, only one Life, one en-

ergy
An endless cosmic ocean, the one divine plan

[Chorus]

Take a deep breath, feel the rhythm inside
Flow with the beat where Love will abide
Come dive with me into the stream of Life
We'll dance through the joy, beyond struggle and
strife

Samadhi – surrender and let it flow
Samadhi – the only thing you need to know
Don't struggle, don't fight, just let it be
Surrender your soul, come dance with me

[Verse 2]

I see you climbing, searching in vain
Chasing the sun, running from the rain
Caught in the mind's endless debate
Lost in tomorrow or yesterday's weight

But Life's not a riddle you have to solve
It's a rhythm where everything evolves
The wave returns to the ocean's embrace
Feel the unity beyond time and space

[Pre-Chorus]

I am the wave and the ocean, the dancer and the
dance
We are one, not two, in every circumstance
There's no beginning, no final breath
Only Life unending – beyond birth and death

[Chorus]

Take a deep breath, feel the rhythm inside
Flow with the beat where Love will abide
Come dive with me into the stream of Life
We'll dance through the joy, beyond struggle and
strife

Samadhi – surrender and let it flow
Samadhi – the only thing you need to know
Don't struggle, don't fight, just let it be
Surrender your soul, come dance with me

[Bridge]

Breathe in Peace, exhale the fear
Feel the flow that brought you here
No need to grasp, no need to hold
In the stream of Life, just let it unfold

The dance goes on, from dusk till dawn
In every heartbeat, we're never gone
One breath, one soul, one sacred way
Together in Samadhi, we'll sway and stay

[Chorus – Extended]

Take a deep breath, feel the rhythm inside
Flow with the beat where Love will abide
Come dive with me into the stream of Life
We'll dance through the joy, beyond struggle and
strife

Samadhi – surrender and let it flow
Samadhi – the only thing you need to know

Don't struggle, don't fight, just let it be
Surrender your soul, come dance with me

[instrumental interlude]

[Bridge]

Breathe in Peace, exhale the fear
Feel the flow that brought you here
No need to grasp, no need to hold
In the stream of Life, just let it unfold

The dance goes on, from dusk till dawn
In every heartbeat, we're never gone
One breath, one soul, one sacred way
Together in Samadhi, we'll sway and stay

[Outro]

Move like the river, flow like the sea
Dance with the stars in perfect harmony
There's no end, no beginning, just the great unseen
Forever we dance in the cosmic dream

Samadhi – flowin' endlessly
Samadhi – come dance with me.

The Wave and the Ocean

There is something ancient in these words. Not just a melody, not just a song – but a remembering. Like something the soul already knows, whispered back to itself in rhythm and rhyme. A soft hymn to the truth we so often forget: That we are not separate. That we are not lost. That we are not alone.

The wave and the ocean – they are not two. They are one motion, one being, one breath moving through many shapes.

And you … you, too, are that wave.

You rise in moments of joy, crash in moments of sorrow, stretch outward in longing, then pull inward in rest.

You shimmer in sunlight and disappear into shadow. And yet, you are never not part of the sea.

> *The wave and the ocean,*
> *they move as one…"*

These lines don't ask you to believe anything. They ask you to *feel*. Feel the pulse beneath your skin – is it not the same rhythm that moves the tides? Feel the ache of your heart – is it not the same pull that draws the waves back home?

In this song, the ocean is not just water. It is the great mystery, the divine current, the Source that births all things and gathers them again. And the wave? The wave is your story, your form, your journey.

But even as you rise and crash, you have never left the ocean. Not for a single moment.

The Dance of Life, The Rhythm of Return

> *The wave rolls in, the wave rolls out …*
> *Like Life on the journey,*
> *up and down we go.*

Such simplicity. Such truth.

How much effort we spend trying to hold back the tides of change. We want the highs to last forever. We fear the fall, the crash, the letting go. But this song reminds us: it's all part of the rhythm.

There is no shame in rising. There is no shame in falling. Both are part of the dance.

Even the wave that crashes is not lost. It returns, reshaped – but never destroyed. Because in the ocean's heart, *nothing is wasted*. Everything belongs.

And so do you.

Let Go – And Find Yourself in the Flow

Don't hold too tight …
Flow with the current,
you'll find where you belong.

How these lines speak to the grasping mind. We want certainty. We want control. But Life is water – and water cannot be gripped. The tighter we hold, the more it slips through.

But surrender … Surrender is not weakness. It is trust. It is the courage to move with Life instead of against it. To let go of the illusion of separateness and float back into the current that has carried us all along.

> *Oh, wave upon the ocean,*
> *don't fear the tide …*
> *In the depths, Peace will always grow.*

These words are a comfort to the soul caught in the storm. Because, yes – the winds will rise. The sea will rage. But beneath the surface, in the great quiet deep, nothing is disturbed.

There is a place in you like that. A stillness no storm can touch. A depth where fear dissolves, and Peace grows like coral – silent and strong.

This song calls you to that place. Not to escape the surface, but to *anchor* yourself in the knowing that you are held. Always. Already.

A Homecoming in Every Breath

And finally, the song leaves you not with instruction, but with a blessing:

> *So live like a wave,*
> *and love like the sea …*

Live fully. Crash gloriously. Stretch outward with wonder, and retreat with gentleness. Let your days be a dance, not a duty. Let your Love be vast, formless, and free – like the sea that holds the wave, like the Source that holds you.

> *For when the wave meets the ocean's shore,*
> *It returns to the sea, for-evermore.*

You don't need to chase belonging. You are already returning. Even now. Even here.

Let this song be the salt on your skin, the wind in your soul, the tide in your chest.

Let it remind you …

You are the wave.

You are the sea.

You rise, you fall – and you always return

To Love.

To Life.

To the One.

The Lyrics

[Chorus]

The wave and the ocean, they move as one,
Rising with the moon, shining in the sun.
Flowing together, no beginning, no end,
Every wave that crashes will rise again.

[Verse 1]

The wave rolls in, the wave rolls out,
It comes with the rhythm, there's no room for doubt.
Like Life on the journey, up and down we go,
Some days it's fast, some days it's slow.

We are all like waves upon the sea,
Moving through time, just trying to be free.
But every wave returns from where it came,
And in the ocean's heart, we're all the same.

[Chorus]

The wave and the ocean, they move as one,
Rising with the moon, shining in the sun.
Flowing together, no beginning, no end,
Every wave that crashes will rise again.

[Bridge]

Oh, wave upon the ocean, don't fear the tide,
You are the sea, no need to hide.
Though storms may come, and winds may blow,
In the depths, Peace will always grow.

[Verse 2]

When you ride the wave, don't hold too tight,
For nothing lasts, not day or night.
It's all just a dance on the ocean's floor,
And when one ends, there's always more.

We think we're alone, but we are the same,
No wave stands apart, no one to blame.

So let go, surrender to the ocean's song,
Flow with the current, you'll find where you belong.

[Chorus]

The wave and the ocean, they move as one,
Rising with the moon, shining in the sun.
Flowing together, no beginning, no end,
Every wave that crashes will rise again.

[Outro]

So live like a wave, and love like the sea,
Let go of fear, and just let it be.
For when the wave meets the ocean's shore,
It returns to the sea, for-evermore.

Doctor Forest

There is a kind of medicine that doesn't come in bottles, a kind of healing that doesn't wear a white coat or speak in diagnoses. It walks barefoot. It hums in leaves. It speaks in silence and sings with the breeze.

Doctor Forest is not just a song – it is a homecoming. A remembering. An invitation to step out of the spinning mind and into the sanctuary of the living Earth.

It begins, as many soul journeys do, with heaviness. With headaches, heartaches, weariness of the world. With feeling misunderstood. With the dull ache of disconnection – from inspiration, from joy, from self.

And then comes the call – not to a pharmacy, but to the forest. Not to fix, but to listen. Not to numb, but to feel again.

The Story behind the Song

The German poem "*Doktor Wald*" by Helmut Dagenbach describes the healing power of nature, particularly the forest, in a poetic and light-hearted way. It portrays the forest as a doctor who can soothe not just physical ailments like headaches but also emotional burdens, offering relief through fresh air, sunshine, and tranquillity. The poem humorously emphasises that "Doctor Forest" doesn't prescribe pills but instead promotes well-being through connection with nature. It even playfully mentions that, though effective, this doctor doesn't make house calls. – Our lyrics were inspired by the poem, which we quote here in its original form:

> *Wenn ich an Kopfweh leide und Neurosen,*
> *mich unverstanden fühle oder alt,*
> *und mich die holden Musen nicht liebkosen,*
> *dann konsultiere ich den Doktor Wald.*
>
> *Er ist mein Augenarzt und Psychiater,*
> *mein Orthopäde und mein Internist.*

Er hilft mir sicher über jeden Kater,
ob er von Kummer oder Cognac ist.

Er hält nicht viel von Pülverchen und Pille,
doch umso mehr von Luft und Sonnenschein.
Und kaum umfängt mich angenehme Stille,
raunt er mir zu: „Nun atme mal tief ein!"

Ist seine Praxis oft auch überlaufen,
in seiner Obhut läuft man sich gesund.
Und Kreislaufkranke, die noch heute schnaufen,
sind morgen ohne klinischen Befund.

Er bringt uns immer wieder auf die Beine,
das Seelische ins Gleichgewicht,
verhindert Fettansatz und Gallensteine.
nur – Hausbesuche macht er leider nicht.

Where the Trees Become Teachers

> *I call on Doctor Forest,*
> *where healing abounds …*

We don't always know we're sick until we begin to heal. And sometimes the soul aches most not from pain, but from forgetting – forgetting how to breathe, how to pause, how to be.

In the company of trees, we begin to remember.

Doctor Forest prescribes no pills, no potions. Just the original elements – breath, light, silence, Earth.

No dosage.

No warnings.

Only presence.

The rustle of leaves becomes a lullaby. The sun on your face, a warm and wordless embrace. The birds don't ask questions. The moss doesn't judge. The wind does not rush you to be someone else.

The Sacred Simplicity of Air and Light

> He prescribes no pills,
> no powders for me,
> But air and sunlight, wild and free.

So simple. So often overlooked.

And yet – isn't that the mystery? That the things which heal us most are the things we cannot buy or own? The breath. The stillness. The feeling of bark under palm. The way a shaft of light moves through green canopy like stained glass in a cathedral of Life.

This is the temple.

This is the doctor.

This is the sanctuary that was never gone – only waiting.

Surrendering to the Cure That Cannot Be Controlled

> *Even when others crowd his door,*
> *His remedy works for-evermore.*

Nature doesn't need to be efficient. She doesn't mind how many come. Her medicine has no shortage. No waiting list. No expiration date.

She offers herself freely, abundantly. But there's a condition.

You must come as you are. You must come to her.

> *Doctor Forest doesn't do house calls nearby …*

This line, playful as it is, holds deep truth. You can't summon nature into your rush. You must slow down to meet her. You must leave behind the noise, the concrete, the endless scrolling and solving.

You must walk where the trees grow tall. And then, like a child returning to its mother, you remember: You were never sick. You were just out of rhythm.

The Soul's Return to Rhythm

The reggae beat under this song is no accident. It is the rhythm of the Earth. The heartbeat of the soil. The pulse of the sea. It moves through you, not with urgency, but with ease. A pace forgotten by the city. A tempo not of clocks, but of clouds.

And the saxophone … oh, the saxophone. It speaks where words would stumble. It weeps, laughs, and dances – like wind through pine. Like joy rediscovered after a long exile.

> *Doctor Forest, heal me with the breeze …*

Yes. Let the breeze be the balm. Let the scent of damp Earth be the medicine. Let birdsong be the diagnosis: *you are not broken.*

The Final Prescription: Belonging

In the later verses, the healing deepens. We are not just soothed – we are restored.

> *He lifts me up and balances my soul …*

This is the deeper miracle: Not just the end of pain, But the return of balance. Of clarity. Of wholeness.

And not just for the body. But for the mind, the heart, the invisible aches we carry.

> *Teach me to see through open eyes …*

This is the quiet gospel of the forest – that Peace is not somewhere else. That healing is not reserved for the lucky few. It is available, now, in the green hush, In the presence that sees you not as a problem, But as part of the whole.

And in the final lines, the truth is gently laid in our hands:

<blockquote>
So live like a wave, and love like the sea,
Let go of fear, and just let it be …
</blockquote>

Because the forest is not just a place. It is a teacher. A healer. A mirror.

It shows us how to love. How to breathe. How to *be*.

Closing: A Forest Within

As the saxophone fades, as the leaves whisper their closing prayer, something lingers. Not just calm – but *knowing*.

That Doctor Forest is not only found in the woods. He is also within you. In the breath you forgot to notice. In the stillness waiting behind your thoughts. In the pulse of your own heart – which has always, always beaten in time with the Earth.

So go, when you need him. Go where the green knows your name. Where no prescription is needed. Where nothing is asked of you but presence.

And there – beneath branch and sky – Let yourself be healed by the one doctor who charges nothing … yet gives you everything.

Doctor Forest.
Nature's Love.
All you need.

The Lyrics

[Verse 1]

When my head feels heavy and Life's got me down,
When I'm misunderstood, wearing a frown,
When inspiration hides, nowhere to be found,
I call on Doctor Forest, where healing abounds.

He's my eye doctor, my healer inside,
My bones feel stronger with him as my guide.
Whether sorrow or drink caused the pain in my head,
With the forest's Peace, I rise from my bed.

[Chorus]

Doctor Forest, heal me with the breeze,
Sunshine and stillness put my heart at ease.
In your care, I breathe and unwind,
Your Peace restores my soul and mind.
Oh, Doctor Forest, I'm feeling free,
Nature's Love is all I need!

[Bridge 1]

Oh yeah … Nature calling, calling me …
Feel the rhythm of the Earth, feel the breeze …

[Verse 2]

He prescribes no pills, no powders for me,
But air and sunlight, wild and free.
In silence, he whispers, "Take a deep breath,"
In his hands, I forget fear and stress.

Even when others crowd his door,
His remedy works for-evermore.

Heartbeats steady, no illness remains,
Tomorrow I'll walk without aches or chains.

[Chorus]

Doctor Forest, heal me with the breeze,
Sunshine and stillness put my heart at ease.
In your care, I breathe and unwind,
Your Peace restores my soul and mind.
Oh, Doctor Forest, I'm feeling free,
Nature's Love is all I need!

[Bridge 2]

Oh, Doctor Forest, healer of our souls,
With roots so deep, and wisdom that consoles,
You breathe new Life where we've laid waste,
Mend the wounds of this world, in your embrace.

Teach us the strength in silence, the courage to be still,
In your endless arms, let us feel the thrill,
Of Life's great cycle, the rhythm of rebirth,
Remind us, Doctor, of our place on Earth.

[Verse 3]

He lifts me up and balances my soul,
With every breath, I feel whole.
No room for worries, no gallstones to find,
Peace and joy leave troubles behind.

But one thing that makes me sigh,
Doctor Forest doesn't do house calls nearby.
You gotta meet him where the trees grow tall,
In his presence, you'll rise from any fall.

[Chorus]

Doctor Forest, heal me with the breeze,
Sunshine and stillness put my heart at ease.
In your care, I breathe and unwind,
Your Peace restores my soul and mind.
Oh, Doctor Forest, I'm feeling free,
Nature's Love is all I need!

[Verse 4]
Doctor Forest, healer of the heart,
In your arms, all pain departs.
Whispering leaves, ancient and wise,
Teach me to see through open eyes.

[Bridge 2]

Oh, Doctor Forest, healer of our souls,
With roots so deep, and wisdom that consoles,
You breathe new Life where we've laid waste,
Mend the wounds of this world, in your embrace.

Teach us the strength in silence, the courage to be still,
In your endless arms, let us feel the thrill,
Of Life's great cycle, the rhythm of rebirth,
Remind us, Doctor, of our place on Earth.

[Chorus]

Doctor Forest, heal me with the breeze,
Sunshine and stillness put my heart at ease.
In your care, I breathe and unwind,
Your Peace restores my soul and mind.

Oh, Doctor Forest, I'm feeling free,
Nature's Love is all I need!

[Verse 5]

Doctor Forest, where shadows play,
Guide me along your emerald way.
In your roots, I feel the flow,
Connecting all, above and below.

[Final Chorus]

Doctor Forest, heal me with the breeze,
Sunshine and stillness put my heart at ease.
In your care, I breathe and unwind,
Your Peace restores my soul and mind.
Oh, Doctor Forest, I'm feeling free,
Nature's Love is all I need!

[Outro]

Breathe in deep ... and let it all go.
Doctor Forest, your Love will always flow ...

Freedom

There are songs that rouse you to dance. And then there are songs that ask you to listen with your whole being. This one – this one speaks not just to the ears, but to the conscience. To the quiet place inside that holds both longing and responsibility.

> Freedom, oh freedom, it comes with a price ...

The chorus begins not with triumph, but with truth. And that's the heart of it: this is not a song of rebellion. It is a song of remembrance.

Because somewhere along the way, we confused freedom with indulgence. We mistook it for the power to do whatever we want, whenever we want. But this song gently steps in, puts a hand on our shoulder, and says:

> *Freedom ain't just for you – it's for everybody.*

The Echo of Every Action

> *What you give to the world will come back the same.*

This is not karma as punishment. This is interbeing. It's the realisation that we live in a woven world, where no word is wasted, no act is isolated, no decision goes unseen.

You are free – yes. But not free from consequence. You are free *with* consequence.

Like a stone dropped into a still lake, every movement sends out ripples – and those ripples reach shores you may never see.

So the song asks: Will your ripple carry Love, or fear? Compassion, or blame? Healing, or harm?

Freedom's Shadow and Light

> *You're free to speak,*
> *but words can sting …*
>
> *You're free to sit still,*
> *but even that's a choice …*

So often we focus on visible freedoms: To move. To speak. To act. But this song draws us deeper – to the subtle powers, the quiet freedoms that live within:

The freedom to choose kindness instead of reaction.

The freedom to hold space when the world screams.

The freedom to say no – not from fear, but from wisdom.

The freedom to *not participate* in the cycle of hate.

Because freedom is not about doing as we please – it's about choosing what serves the whole.

The River Knows

> *The river runs free, but it shapes the land …*

This image is everything.

Yes, the river flows – wild, free, alive. But wherever it goes, it leaves a mark. It carves canyons. It nourishes valleys. It floods and it quenches.

So too with us. Our freedom leaves footprints. The way we love, the way we spend, the way we listen – it all shapes the landscape of the world we share.

Are we leaving scars … or gardens?

The Sacred Gift of Responsibility

> *Freedom's a gift, but it's also a key …*

A key opens something. A key invites you in. This song reminds us that freedom is not an escape hatch – it's an invitation into maturity. A sacred trust.

To live with freedom is to live with awareness. To move not like a wrecking ball, but like a healer with hands open. To leave a trail of dignity behind us, not damage.

Legacy in the Wind

> *Leave a legacy of Love behind …*

This line lands gently – like a prayer whispered to the soul. We will not live forever. But our choices echo.

The freedom we claim today builds the world our children will inherit. Our tone, our silence, our laughter, our laws – they become the atmosphere in which others must breathe.

This song – with its reggae roots, its wise rhythm – is not shouting. It's inviting. Inviting us to slow down, to feel the weight of our freedom, and to carry it with Love.

Not as a burden. But as a *blessing*. As a sacred instrument of Peace.

Closing Reflection: The Dance of Discernment

So yes – dance. But dance with awareness. Dance knowing the ground you dance upon is shared. Speak your truth – but with a tone that others can survive. Move like a river – but remember the banks.

Because freedom without Love is just impulse. And freedom without wisdom is just noise. But freedom with Love … Freedom with wisdom … That is sacred. That is powerful. That is the kind of freedom that lifts *everybody*.

Let this song remind you:

You are free. You are powerful. You are responsible.

Use it well. Use it kindly. Use it to bless the world

The Lyrics

[Chorus]

Freedom, oh freedom, it comes with a price,
Every step you take, gotta think twice.
The choices you make, they shape who you be,
Freedom ain't just for you, it's for everybody.

[Verse 1]

You say you're free, and you wanna run wild,
Do what you like, live free like a child.
But freedom, my friend, it ain't just a game,
What you give to the world will come back the same.

When you act from Love, you make the world bright,
But if you plant hate, don't expect no light.
So take it easy, and tread with care,
Every action you take, it's felt everywhere.

[Chorus]

Freedom, oh freedom, it comes with a price,
Every step you take, gotta think twice.
The choices you make, they shape who you be,
Freedom ain't just for you, it's for everybody.

[Bridge]

The river runs free, but it shapes the land,
Every twist and turn leaves a mark on the sand.
So move as you will, but know this for true,
The world you create will reflect back on you.

[Verse 2]

True freedom's not only doing your will,
It's knowing that actions can heal or kill.
You're free to speak, but words can sting,
They fly through the air and change everything.

You're free to sit still, but even that's a choice,
In the silence, you hold a powerful voice.

Freedom is deep, it's not just a dance,
It's knowing when to act, when to give Life a chance.

[Chorus]

Freedom, oh freedom, it comes with a price,
Every step you take, gotta think twice.
The choices you make, they shape who you be,
Freedom ain't just for you, it's for everybody.

[Outro]

So live with intention, be wise and kind,
Leave a legacy of Love behind.
Freedom's a gift, but it's also a key,
Unlock the world with responsibility.

The Monkeys' Song

The Story behind the Song

There is a large group of vervet monkeys that visits my garden regularly. They come searching for food, play-ing among the trees and flowers … and they are end-lessly curious. They watch us closely, peeking through the windows of the house, often spending long mo-ments observing me as I work in my office.

When I look into their eyes, I feel as if they are reflecting on what they see – not just watching, but wondering.

In our garden, they are welcome. There is mutual respect. We see the monkeys, and the monkeys see us.

But outside this peaceful space, the world is a much harsher place for them. They are struck by cars, electrocuted by fences, and killed – sometimes even out of so-called "fun". People beat them, rob them of their freedom, or drive them away with stones, seeing them only as pests.

I often wonder what they think. How they feel about this world we've made.

At last, I've found the story I believe I see in their eyes when they look at me.

This is their song.

Some songs don't just sing – they speak. Some lyrics aren't crafted from dreams, but from the raw wound of a world in crisis. And sometimes, the voices you thought were silent – the animals, the trees, the forgotten Earth – rise up in rhythm and rhyme and look straight into your soul.

"The Monkeys' Song" is not a lullaby. It is not a song of comfort. It is a mirror. A jungle mirror, woven with vines, laced with smoke, reflecting back the madness of modern humanity from a height we forgot to look up to.

They See What We Don't See

There is a sacred irony here. We, the "civilised," the "developed", the "intelligent", live heads-down in screens, lost in the buzz of machines. But the monkeys – wild, playful, instinctual – see everything. They live where our ancestors once walked barefoot. They swing from the limbs of the Mother while we bulldoze her to dust.

And they are watching.

Not with hatred. Not with vengeance. But with a wisdom older than our skyscrapers. With an understanding we traded for steel and gold.

The Crown of Creation – Bent and Bloodied

You call yourself the crown of creation, but how?

This refrain hits like a drumbeat of truth.

Yes, we call ourselves the peak. The pinnacle of evolution. We write poetry and launch satellites. But at what cost?

The monkeys have a question – a sacred question: If you are the crown, then why does your reign smell like smoke? Why do rivers choke and forests fall at the wave of your royal hand?

What kind of king burns his own kingdom?

Laughter From the Treetops

> *But we're laughing,*
> *oh yes, we're laughing inside …*

This laughter is not cruel. It is ancient. It is the kind of laughter that knows better than to cling to illusions. The monkeys laugh not because they're mocking – But because they understand what we forgot:

That empires fall. That greed devours its own children. That the Earth outlasts its abusers.

They wait not in powerlessness, but in *patience*. Because while we scramble for profit, They swing in rhythm with the pulse of the planet.

You Say We're Wild

> *You say we are the animals, wild and*
> *free …*
> *But who's the real prisoner, can't you*
> *see?*

Here lies the haunting beauty of the song: the role reversal.

We thought cages were for beasts. But look closer – who is caged?

We lock animals in zoos, but cannot leave our own digital prisons. We claim dominion, yet cannot stop consuming. We chase freedom, yet live chained to our devices, our debt, our illusions.

The monkeys ask without malice: Who is really lost?

They do not need gadgets.

They do not crave conquest.

They do not kill for sport.

Yet we call them primitive.

Waiting in the Trees

> *Let us wait and see,*
> *oh brothers and sisters …*

They do not fight us. They do not march or vote or shout. They simply *wait*. And in that waiting is a kind of faith – not in us, necessarily, but in the laws of Life.

Because the Earth remembers. The soil keeps score. And every forest burned is a breath we won't get back.

Yet still – they wait. They witness.

And when we are gone, when the lights die out, they will still be singing in the trees.

The Final Word is Love

> *We live with the Earth,*
> *we know how to love.*

This isn't a song of revenge. It's a *lament*. A teaching.

It's the voice of Life reminding us: We were never meant to rule. We were meant to *belong*.

We were meant to live in relationship – with the rivers, the roots, the creatures who dance without needing a reason.

We have tried to conquer the world. But perhaps the monkeys – wild, laughing, wise – have always known the deeper truth:

That Love is not something you take. It's something you live.

Who Will Be Laughing in the End?

> *The monkeys are here.*
> *The monkeys are wise.*
> *We'll swing in the trees as your empire*
> *dies.*

This song is not just a warning. It is a poem from the lungs of the forest. It is the prophecy of the watchers. It is a reggae elegy for the Anthropocene.

And as the final chorus fades into wind and vine, the question lingers like a sacred echo:

Who is truly evolved? Who knows how to live? And who – in the end – will be laughing?

Let us wait and see.

The Lyrics

[Intro]

Ooooh, ooooh, ooooh, yeah, yeah, yeah
Look at them now, look at them now
Monkeys on the tree, we see what you don't see
We see what you don't see...

[Chorus]

Hey, you humans, what you doing now?
You call yourself the crown of creation, but how?
You destroy our home, you poison the land,
But we're watching you closely, so understand,

Let us wait and see, oh brothers and sisters,
Let us wait and see, yeah, who'll be the winners.

[Verse 1]

Up in the trees, we swing and we play,
We see your machines tearing forests away,
You cut down our homes for your paper and greed,
While our family's crying, left with nothing to feed.

You crush us with cars, you trap us in chains,
Beat us, enslave us, it's all in your name.
But we're laughing, oh yes, we're laughing inside,
For your greed and your arrogance will be your own
tide.

[Chorus]

Hey, you humans, what you doing now?
You call yourself the crown of creation, but how?

You destroy our home, you poison the land,
But we're watching you closely, so understand,

Let us wait and see, oh brothers and sisters,
Let us wait and see, yeah, who'll be the winners.

[Verse 2]

You claim dominion over Earth and sky,
But look at your world, can you tell me why?
The rivers are dying, the oceans turn black,
You choke on your smoke, but you never look back.

You chase after money, like it's all that you need,
While your heart grows hollow from the sickness of greed.
And we see you, from the treetops so high,
Oh, the monkeys are laughing, while you live in a lie.

[Bridge]

Oooh, oooh, we see it all, yeah, yeah,
You're lost in your madness, trapped in your fear.
You say we are the animals, wild and free,
But who's the real prisoner, can't you see?

Money is your master, power your chain,
You fight for control, but you're losing your reign.

[Chorus]

Hey, you humans, what you doing now?
You call yourself the crown of creation, but how?
You destroy our home, you poison the land,
But we're watching you closely, so understand,

Let us wait and see, oh brothers and sisters,
Let us wait and see, yeah, who'll be the winners.

[Verse 3]

We see you digging, drilling the ground,
For treasures that bring your own ruin around.
You're slaves to your gadgets, trapped in your screens,
While the Earth cries out and the forest screams.

You poison the air, you poison the soil,
And still you believe you're the kings of it all.
But we're patient, we wait, we swing from our vines,
While your empire crumbles, we'll be just fine.

[Chorus]

Hey, you humans, what you doing now?
You call yourself the crown of creation, but how?
You destroy our home, you poison the land,
But we're watching you closely, so understand,

Let us wait and see, oh brothers and sisters,
Let us wait and see, yeah, who'll be the winners.

[Bridge]

Oh, we're the monkeys, watching from above,
We live with the Earth, we know how to love.
We don't need your cities, your gold, or your war,
We dance with the wind, we're free at the core.

[Chorus]

Hey, you humans, what you doing now?
You call yourself the crown of creation, but how?

You destroy our home, you poison the land,
But we're watching you closely, so understand,

Let us wait and see, oh brothers and sisters,
Let us wait and see, yeah, who'll be the winners.

[Bridge]

Oh, we're the monkeys, watching from above,
We live with the Earth, we know how to love.
We don't need your cities, your gold, or your war,
We dance with the wind, we're free at the core.

You say we're primitive, but maybe you're blind,
Who's truly evolved, who's lost their own mind?

[Chorus]

Hey, you humans, what you doing now?
You call yourself the crown of creation, but how?
You destroy our home, you poison the land,
But we're watching you closely, so understand,

Let us wait and see, oh brothers and sisters,
Let us wait and see, yeah, who'll be the winners.

[Outro]

Ooooh, ooooh, yeah, yeah, yeah
Let us wait and see, let us wait and see,
Who will be laughing in the end, you or we?

The monkeys are here, the monkeys are wise,
We'll swing in the trees as your empire dies.

Let us wait and see, oh brothers and sisters,
Let us wait and see, yeah, who'll be the winners.

[Fade Out]

Hey, you humans, what you doing now?
Look around you, it's crumbling down.
The monkeys are laughing, the Earth sings her song,
Maybe it's you who didn't belong …

68

Karma Comes Back

Some songs arrive like waves, gently reminding us of truths we already know but often forget. "Karma Comes Back" is one such song – simple in melody, yet profound in message. It is not a warning. It is not a threat. It is a mirror, softly held up to the soul.

In its steady rhythm and grounded wisdom, the song whispers what sages have said across time and continents:

Nothing we do is ever truly lost. Each thought, each word, each deed – it ripples out. And eventually, it returns.

Every Seed You Plant

> *Karma comes back, round and round it go,*
> *Every seed you plant is the one you sow.*

The chorus is a mantra – a spiritual law wrapped in reggae rhythm.

Life is not random. It is relational. And though the world may appear chaotic, behind the surface moves a quiet justice – not punitive, but organic. Just as a mango seed grows a mango tree, just as water flows downhill, so too does energy return to its source.

Karma is not about punishment or reward. It's about consequence. It's about *connection*. It's about remembering that we are not isolated actors on a disconnected stage – we are threads in a living tapestry. What we touch, we alter.

And the imprint we leave on the world is the path we walk tomorrow.

The Mirror of Life

This verse speaks directly to the soul that forgets. To the part of us that acts in haste, reacts in anger, or chooses convenience over care.

But Life remembers. Not with bitterness – but with precision.

Life is a mirror – not because it wants to punish, but because it wants to teach. And every time we look away from that reflection, Life gently turns our face back toward it.

The world reflects not only what we do – but who we are becoming. Karma is not just what returns to us – it's also what we turn into.

The Flow Cannot Be Denied

This image is beautiful. A river doesn't stop to argue. It doesn't demand your belief. It just flows.

We can dam it. We can try to divert it. But eventually, it finds its way. And so too does karma.

Whether in this moment or a hundred days from now, what we pour into the world eventually fills our own cup.

So let the waters we pour be pure. Let them quench and cleanse, not drown or poison.

Invisible Intentions, Visible Effects

> *It's not just in words, but the thoughts*
> *in your head,*
> *What you wish for others comes back*
> *instead.*

This verse takes us deeper – into the *interior world*. Because karma isn't just about outward action – it begins within.

We may never speak the bitterness we carry. We may never act on the resentment we hold. But energy moves in silence, too.

The universe listens to the hidden places of the heart.

Which is why forgiveness isn't just for others – it's for us.

Which is why compassion isn't weakness – it's protection.

What we wish upon others becomes the atmosphere we breathe.

Let your inner weather be kind.

Each Moment, a Rewrite

> *Every moment is a chance to rewrite the song …*

Here is the grace of it all. Karma is not a rigid sentence – it's a living melody. We can always sing a different verse. We can always shift the tune.

We are never locked in our past. Each new breath is a doorway. Each choice, a brushstroke on the painting of our Life.

This line reminds us: we are both the cause and the correction. And it's never too late to choose again.

The Final Offering: A Life of Love

> *So live in truth, be kind and wise,*
> *Look with compassion through open*
> *eyes.*

As the song winds down, it offers not a conclusion, but a direction.

To live in truth – not in appearances. To be kind – not only when it is easy. To see through eyes that do not judge first, but understand.

In the circle of karma, everything returns. But when Love is what you give, Love is what surrounds you. And in that Love, the cycle becomes not a trap – but a dance.

"Karma Comes Back" is a compass song. It doesn't demand obedience. It invites awareness.

Not through fear, but through understanding. That what you do matters. That how you think matters. That the world you shape shapes you back.

It reminds us that the spiritual path is not some distant mountaintop – it's right here, in how we treat the stranger, in how we respond to anger, in how we speak when no one is listening.

Karma is not cosmic revenge. It is cosmic rhythm. A sacred echo of your own voice in the song of the universe.

So walk with care. Speak with light. Love with both hands open.

Because yes – karma comes back. But so does grace. So does healing. So does joy, when joy is what you give.

Let this song be your reminder:

You are the cause.

You are the seed.

You are the song.

Sing it well.

The Lyrics

[Chorus]

Karma comes back, round and round it go,
Every seed you plant is the one you sow.
Good or bad, it's a circle of Life,
What you send out comes back, day or night.

[Verse 1]

You think you can hide from the things that you do,
But every step you take leaves a mark on you.
Life is a mirror, reflecting it all,
No act too big, no deed too small.

If you give Love, it will follow your way,
If you bring harm, there's a price to pay.
So be wise in your actions, walk steady and sure,
Karma's a river, you can't ignore.

[Chorus]

Karma comes back, round and round it go,
Every seed you plant is the one you sow.
Good or bad, it's a circle of Life,
What you send out comes back, day or night.

[Bridge]

The winds will change, the tides will turn,
Every flame you spark will one day burn.
You can't outrun what the universe tracks,
Sooner or later, karma comes back.

[Verse 2]

It's not just in words, but the thoughts in your head,
What you wish for others comes back instead.
If you spread joy, then joy you'll meet,
But if you spread pain, it returns to your feet.

Every moment is a chance to rewrite the song,
To choose the right path, not the wrong.
So tread with Love, make Peace your way,
For karma's watching every night and day.

[Chorus]

Karma comes back, round and round it go,
Every seed you plant is the one you sow.
Good or bad, it's a circle of Life,
What you send out comes back, day or night.

[Outro]

So live in truth, be kind and wise,
Look with compassion through open eyes.
What you do to others reflects on you,
In the circle of karma, it's all true.

Donkey's Song

Some songs don't dazzle. They don't soar with glamour or race with speed. They walk – steady, honest, with hooves that know the dust of the road and a soul that sings not of victory, but of *service*.

"Donkey's Song" is one such hymn.

It carries the wisdom of the overlooked. The patient strength of the humble. The dignity of those who carry the world without demanding applause.

It is not the song of the stallion, the lion, or the eagle – It is the song of the donkey. And in its rhythm, there is something holy.

Slow and Strong

> I'm just a donkey, slow and strong,
> Walking steady, singing my song.

From the very first line, there is no pretence. No need to impress. No hunger to compete. Only a clear and open heart, doing what needs to be done – step by step.

In a world that worships speed, flash, and ambition, this song reminds us of another way: The way of consistency. Of groundedness. Of knowing that meaning isn't found in the applause, but in the doing.

The donkey doesn't rush – because the donkey doesn't need to. The destination is not as important as the integrity of the journey.

Steady Beats the Heart That Serves

> Though the road is rough,
> and the hills are steep,
> I carry my load and never miss a beat.

Life, in its essence, is not smooth. The terrain is uneven. Some days ask more than others. Some burdens feel heavier than what we think we can bear.

But the donkey doesn't collapse under hardship. It doesn't resist the road. It accepts what is given, walks what is placed before it, and meets the steep path with sure footing.

There is something deeply sacred in that: Not endurance as martyrdom, but endurance as devotion.

The Strength of the Undervalued

> *They laugh and call me foolish and slow*

Mockery is often the language of misunderstanding. The world may laugh at slowness, at silence, at the ones who don't shine.

But the donkey knows something deeper: That strength isn't measured in noise. That wisdom isn't found in haste.

> *You ride high today, but wait and see —*
> *When troubles come, you'll call on me.*

Yes. Because when the glitter falls away, when the carriage breaks, when the path gets rough – it's the donkey you turn to. Not the fastest, but the faithful. Not the most praised, but the present.

Nothing to Prove, Everything to Give

> *Slow and steady is the way I move,*
> *No need to rush, got nothing to prove.*

This may be the most radical line in the entire song.

In a world built on proving – proving your worth, proving your value, proving your place – The donkey simply *is*.

And in being what it is – honest, slow, strong, grounded – it becomes indispensable.

The donkey does not complain. It does not show off. But it shows *up*.

And sometimes, that's all that's needed.

Bearing the Burden with Grace

> *Every burden I bear, I bear with grace,*
> *It's not about the prize,*
> *it's about the pace.*

Here we meet the essence of true service. To carry what Life gives – not with complaint, but with dignity. To measure progress not by speed, but by faithfulness. To know that real grace is not flashy – it's quiet. It's reliable.

This is where the donkey becomes more than just an animal – It becomes a symbol. A reflection of the kind of strength the world forgets to honour.

And in the lines that follow, it becomes even more:

> *Even when you stumble, I won't let you*
> *fall.*
> *For patience and strength will see me*
> *through —*
> *I'll carry the weight, I'll carry you too.*

What deeper Love is there than this? To carry not just burdens, but *each other*?

This is what elders do. This is what mothers and fathers do. This is what the Earth herself does.

Be Like the Donkey

> *So be like the donkey, humble and true,*
> *Do what you must, and see it through.*

In the end, the donkey is not asking us to become less. It's asking us to remember what truly *matters*:

To be *reliable*.

To be *present*.

To act with *purpose*.

To live without needing to be *seen*.

This song does not dazzle – it *grounds*. It reminds us that success is not found in how far you run, but in how fully you show up. That faithfulness, humility, and quiet strength are not outdated virtues – they are *foundations* for a better world.

Final Reflection: The Quiet Nobility of the Donkey's Path

"Donkey's Song" is a quiet revolution. It stands at the edge of the fast-paced world and says: slow down. It stands in the noise and says: be still. It stands in the race and says: walk steady.

The donkey has no throne. But it has *honour*. It carries burdens others cast off. It bears the weight of generations – with a song in its heart and no need for glory.

So today – maybe don't be the lion, the hawk, the racehorse. Maybe be the donkey.

Carry what matters.

Move with care.

Love with action.

And let the song you sing be steady, soft, and strong.

Because in the end, when the day is done and the dust settles, the ones who walked with quiet grace will be the ones who carried the world.

The Lyrics

[Chorus]

I'm just a donkey, slow and strong,
Walking steady, singing my song.
Though the road is rough, and the hills are steep,
I carry my load and never miss a beat.

[Verse 1]

They laugh and call me foolish and slow,
But I take my time, and I always know,
Every step forward, no matter how small,
Is better than running and losing it all.

I don't need glory, I don't need fame,
I work with purpose, no shame in my name.
You ride high today, but wait and see,
When troubles come, you'll call on me.

[Chorus]

I'm just a donkey, slow and strong,
Walking steady, singing my song.
Though the road is rough, and the hills are steep,
I carry my load and never miss a beat.

[Bridge]

Slow and steady is the way I move,
No need to rush, got nothing to prove.
Life's not a race, it's a long old track,
What you send out will come right back.

[Verse 2]

Some dream of riches, some dream of speed,
But I take pride in meeting the need.
Every burden I bear, I bear with grace,
It's not about the prize, it's about the pace.

So laugh if you want, I don't mind at all,
Even when you stumble, I won't let you fall.
For patience and strength will see me through,
I'll carry the weight, I'll carry you too.

[Chorus]

I'm just a donkey, slow and strong,
Walking steady, singing my song.

Though the road is rough, and the hills are steep,
I carry my load and never miss a beat.

[Outro]

So be like the donkey, humble and true,
Do what you must, and see it through.
For Life's not about how fast you run,
It's about the journey when the day is done.

Pilipili

The Story behind the Song

Pilipili is the Swahili word for spicy chilli.

There are dishes that look absolutely delicious – they smell incredible, rich with flavour and promise. But then you take a bite … and suddenly, it feels like your mouth is on fire, your heart skips a beat, and your breath gets stuck in your throat.

I truly love spices and herbs – they give Life to food. But when it comes to hot spicy, I quickly reach my limit.

Living in a country where some restaurants prepare Indian or Arab dishes so hot that you can't taste anything beyond the burn … well, that can be quite a challenge for me.

After one of those fiery restaurant visits, the idea for this song was born.

There are songs that speak of Life with elegance. And then there are songs like *"Pilipili"* – that *taste* of Life. That sting and soothe, that burn and bless. A song you don't just hear – you feel on the tongue, in the belly, and deep in the chest where memory meets meaning.

"Pilipili" – meaning "spicy chilli" – becomes, in this anthem, a metaphor for the flavour of existence. For every sharp turn, every bittersweet memory, every hardship that sears and every joy that dances. It reminds us that the fire in the food is the same fire that fuels the spirit.

This is not just a song about chilli. It is a song about Life, and all its heat.

When Every Bite Burns – and You Keep Eating Anyway

> *Every bite's a flame,*
> *Every taste takes flight.*
> *It's burning wild, but I can't resist …*

Isn't that what Life so often feels like? Too intense, too much – and yet, irresistible. We crave it. We chase it. We return to it, even when it burns.

This is the first lesson of *"Pilipili"*: *Pain and pleasure are never far apart.* They often arrive together, like lovers in disguise. We wince … and we laugh. We cry … and we reach for another bite.

This song celebrates that paradox – that beauty often stings, and pain can carry flavour too.

Sweet, Spicy, and Real

> *It's sweet and spicy, I can't let it go,*
> *But my tongue's on fire, breathing gets slow …*

This is a dance between delight and discomfort. The kind of sensation that makes you feel alive. The kind of Love that's not easy, but unforgettable.

It reminds us that being human means walking through fire and fragrance all at once – and learning to dance in the heat.

You don't numb it. You don't run. You sip *water*, breathe, and keep on moving.

Life is Not a Mild Dish

> *Some dream of riches,*
> *Some dream of speed,*
> *But I take pride in meeting the need …*

This verse moves from the sensory to the spiritual. The speaker is not just eating food – they're living with purpose. They're tasting Life with all its intensity, not to conquer it, but to understand it. To honour it.

Just like *pilipili*, Life isn't always gentle. But gentleness isn't always what the soul needs. Sometimes, it's the burn that purifies. The challenge that awakens courage. The heat that melts away the ego and reveals strength underneath.

Fire as Transformation

> *Life shakes me like chilli in my veins,*
> *But strength inside helps me break the*
> *chains.*

This is not just fire for fire's sake. This is fire as alchemy. As the sacred flame that doesn't destroy, but refines. Burns away the false, and uncovers the true.

In the heat of struggle, the speaker doesn't collapse – he rises. He becomes clearer, stronger, more alive. It's not about avoiding discomfort – it's about finding meaning within it.

Joy Wrapped in Pain

> It's Love in a bite, joy wrapped in pain …

This single line may hold the heart of the song. Life doesn't come in neat packages. It is not either joy *or* sorrow – it is often both, layered, tangled, inseparable.

Love will ache. Dreams will sting. But in the end, we come back for more – not because we enjoy the pain, but because the richness is worth it.

It's the fullness that calls us. The fire that makes the flavour bloom.

Spices of the Soul

> Life is a curry, flavours clash and
> blend …
> Sweet moments balance the heat
> we bear …

There's a deep wisdom here: that our lives are not made of perfect harmony – but of contrast.

What gives Life its taste are the tensions: The sour and the sweet. The bitter and the bold. The laughter that follows grief, the silence that follows a song.

It's the combination – the courage to feel it all – that gives Life its richness.

Pilipili becomes not just food, but philosophy. Not just chilli, but truth.

To Burn and Still Sing

> The burn keeps me alive,
> It's part of the deal!

This is the final acceptance – not resignation, but celebration.

Yes, Life burns.

Yes, some days feel too much.

Yes, the heat will make you cry.

But you still *sing*. You still laugh through the tears. You still rise in the morning, open your heart again, and say:

"Bring me the spice. I'm here for all of it."

That is the soul of this song. Not denial. Not escape. But *wholehearted embrace*.

Closing Reflection: Savour the Fire, Sip the Water, Sing the Song

"*Pilipili*" reminds us that Life is not meant to be bland. It is not meant to be safe and flavourless.

It is meant to be *felt* – deeply, fully, courageously.

There is no guarantee that the spice won't sting. But there *is* the guarantee that you'll grow stronger because of it. And wiser. And more grateful – not just for the sweetness, but for the fire that helped you feel it.

So the next time Life burns your tongue, makes your eyes tear up, or overwhelms your senses – Don't run. Don't curse the spice.

And in that going on, something powerful awakens:

A deeper resilience.

A bolder Love.

A song rising from the heat.

Pilipili.

The flavour of Life.

The heat that heals.

The burn that blesses.

The Lyrics

[Verse 1]

I was waiting, dreaming 'bout this plate,
Mouth was watering, couldn't hardly wait.
Now it's here, but I'm caught in a fight,
Every bite's a flame, every taste takes flight.
It's burning wild, but I can't resist,
So much flavour, like a fiery kiss.

[Chorus]

Pilipili, spices of Life,
Hot like pepper, cut like a knife.
When it burns and the heat's too strong,
I close my eyes, sip water, Life goes on.

[Verse 2]

It's sweet and spicy, I can't let it go,
But my tongue's on fire, breathing gets slow.
I laugh through the tears, what a crazy ride,
The pain and the pleasure, walking side by side.
What do I do? The burn's deep inside,
Sip some water, let the fire subside.

[Chorus]

Pilipili, spices of Life,
Hot like pepper, cut like a knife.
When it burns and the heat's too strong,
I close my eyes, sip water, Life goes on.

[Verse 3]

Sometimes the taste is bitter and rough,
Days get heavy, the road feels tough.
Life shakes me like chilli in my veins,
But strength inside helps me break the chains.
No storm too fierce, no flame too high,
I'll keep my head up, let my spirit fly.

[Chorus]

Pilipili, spices of Life,
Hot like pepper, cut like a knife.

When it burns and the heat's too strong,
I close my eyes, sip water, Life goes on.

[Verse 4]

Sweat drips down, breath running thin,
Like fire within, burning deep in my skin.
Some moments feel like they'll never end,
But every challenge's just a lesson, my friend.
I ride the waves, through storm or sun,
Every day I rise; the journey's not done.

[Bridge]

Oh, the heat makes me dance, makes me sweat,
A taste I won't forgive, and never forget.
It's Love in a bite, joy wrapped in pain,
I take it all in, through sunshine and rain.
No turning back, gotta savor the thrill,
The burn keeps me alive, it's part of the deal!

[Chorus]

Pilipili, spices of Life,
Hot like pepper, cut like a knife.
When it burns and the heat's too strong,
I close my eyes, sip water, Life goes on.

[Verse 5]

Life is a curry, flavours clash and blend,
Joy and struggle mix 'round every bend.
Sometimes the heat will make you fall,
But Love and courage will answer the call.
Like a meal that's bold, I taste it all,
Stand tall, no fear when troubles crawl.

[Chorus]

Pilipili, spices of Life,
Hot like pepper, cut like a knife.
When it burns and the heat's too strong,
I close my eyes, sip water, Life goes on.

[Verse 6]

Oceans rise, deserts dry, seasons spin,
I find my rhythm and dance within.
The heat of trials melts away my doubt,
I sing through the fire, let my soul shout.
Sweet moments balance the heat we bear,
Spices of Life bring meaning we share.

[Bridge]

Oh, the heat makes me dance, makes me sweat,
A taste I won't forgive, and never forget.
It's Love in a bite, joy wrapped in pain,
I take it all in, through sunshine and rain.
No turning back, gotta savour the thrill,
The burn keeps me alive, it's part of the deal!

[Chorus]

Pilipili, spices of Life,
Hot like pepper, cut like a knife.
When it burns and the heat's too strong,
I close my eyes, sip water, Life goes on.

[Verse 7]

Like chilli and lime, Life's not always sweet,
But every taste makes my heart complete.

Through ups and downs, I play my part,
With every spice, I feed my heart.
Though some are hot and make me cry,
I sip my water, and let storms pass by.

[Bridge]

Oh, the heat makes me dance, makes me sweat,
A taste I won't forgive, and never forget.
It's Love in a bite, joy wrapped in pain,
I take it all in, through sunshine and rain.
No turning back, gotta savour the thrill,
The burn keeps me alive, it's part of the deal!

[Chorus]

Pilipili, spices of Life,
Hot like pepper, cut like a knife.
When it burns and the heat's too strong,
I close my eyes, sip water, Life goes on.

[Outro]

Pilipili, Pilipili, spices unfold,
Stories of Life, lessons untold.
When the heat comes, and things feel wrong,
I close my eyes, sip water, Life goes on.

Pilipili, oh Pilipili,
Life's a dish, sometimes tricky.
Through every burn, I sing my song,
I close my eyes, sip water, Life goes on.

Beach Party

Some songs aren't just about music – they are about moments. Moments where the senses awaken, where the world softens its edges, and where joy, nature, and desire melt into one flowing rhythm.

"Beach Party" is one of those songs. It begins gently, like the first breeze of evening, and soon builds into something more – a pulse, a celebration, a memory that smells of salt, glows like gold, and tastes like heat.

At its heart, this is a song about being alive. And deeper still – about the subtle, erotic magic that simmers just beneath the surface of such nights.

The Private Spark Before the Flame

> *Let's have a party, just you and me,*
> *Down by the shore, where the waves*
> *are free.*

The song begins not with a crowd, but with *two*. There's intimacy here – a secret world carved out. A knowing look, a private rhythm, the playful anticipation of what the night might hold.

Before it becomes a party, it's a *seduction*.

This isn't just about fun – it's about chemistry. Two bodies moving closer with each beat, the ocean as witness, the sand a silent bed of invitation. It's the prelude to connection – not yet spoken, but already felt in the sway of hips and the curl of smiles.

From Solitude to Celebration

> *Soon others come, drawn by the beat*

And then the moment expands. The music becomes magnetic. Others arrive, drawn by the invisible pull of freedom and firelight.

What started as personal becomes communal. And yet – the original flame between the two remains intact, glowing quietly even as laughter and movement swirl around.

This is the paradox the song holds beautifully: To lose yourself in the rhythm with others, while still keeping the spark of intimacy alive beneath it all.

It is the art of dancing in a crowd, and still feeling like you're the only two on Earth.

Bodies, Rhythm, and the Joy of Embodiment

> *The sand's alive, our bodies all move,*
> *In the golden hour, we find our groove.*

Here the song celebrates something many overlook: The wisdom of the body. The way joy lives in the hips, the heartbeat, the sway of shoulders under a sky that doesn't judge.

This is not performance – it's *presence*. It's sensual, yes – but also innocent. Eroticism here is not shameful. It's part of being real, open, whole.

Every grain of sand becomes part of the rhythm. Every beat of the drum is an invitation: Feel. Move. Let go.

The Erotic Heartbeat Beneath the Moonlight

> *But when the crowd drifts away,*
> *It's time to be free,*

> *Behind the old tree,*
> *Just you and me.*

And now we return to where it all began – but the energy has shifted.

The sun has set. The stars have opened their eyes. The crowd has faded. And what remains is the simmering afterglow.

This is not just a party any more – it's a moment of surrender.

Behind that old tree – a symbolic veil of privacy – something unspoken takes form. Desire is no longer hidden in the dance. Now it flows freely – in touch, in laughter, in closeness that needs no words.

It's erotic, yes – but in the way that nature is erotic: Honest, warm, unashamed.

More Than a Memory – A Sacred Encounter

> *So here's to the night and the waves'*
> *soft hum,*
> *To the sweetest beach party, more to*
> *come.*

As the song ends, we're left not with closure, but with continuation.

Because real connection – especially when rooted in joy and sensual truth – doesn't end when the music fades. It lingers in the skin. It hums in the breath. It whispers in memory.

The erotic story here is not a tale of conquest or escape. It's about being met – fully, naturally, in the golden light of shared presence.

The beach becomes not just a place of dance, but a sacred space of embodiment. The congas echo the heartbeat. The waves reflect the soul. And the lovers? They become part of the song itself.

Closing Reflection: Dancing Barefoot with Life

"Beach Party" is more than a soundtrack to summer. It's a celebration of Life's sensual rhythm. Of connection that starts with a glance and ends with the stars. Of music that carries us into our bodies, and into each other.

It reminds us:

That joy is holy.

That the body is wise.

That Love, when danced freely, becomes *prayer*.

So let the sand be your dance-floor. Let the night be your veil. Let desire move like the tide – playful, powerful, and perfectly at home.

And when the world fades away…

May it always be just you and me

Behind that old tree.

The Lyrics

[Verse 1]

Let's have a party, just you and me,
Down by the shore, where the waves are free.
Golden light shinin' as the sun dips low,
The sea's a mirror, casting a warm, sweet glow.

We laugh and sway, our feet in the sand,
A secret dance, just you and me hand in hand.

[Chorus]

Oh, beach party, under the sky so wide,
Feel that ocean rhythm, feel the rising tide.
The world fades away, it's just you and me,
Until the music calls the whole party to be.

[Verse 2]

Soon others come, drawn by the beat,
Jumpin' and swingin', feelin' that heat.
Toes in the water, waves hummin' a song,
The vibe so right, can't help but come along.

The sand's alive, our bodies all move,
In the golden hour, we find our groove.

[Chorus]

Oh, beach party, under the sky so wide,
Feel that ocean rhythm, feel the rising tide.
The world fades away, it's just you and me,
But now everybody's part of the party at sea.

[Bridge]

Fresh breeze blowin', salt in the air,
Sun dips lower, a perfect pair.
Each wave a heartbeat, the night's comin' slow,
In this moment, our spirits flow.

[Verse 3]

Now we're swayin' under the stars above,
Everyone's feelin' that reggae Love.
Laughin' and singin', we're all one tribe,
Dancin' together in a natural vibe.

But when the crowd drifts away, it's time to be free,
Behind the old tree, just you and me.

[Chorus]

Oh, beach party, we're the last to stay,
Under moonlight magic, we'll dance and play.
The world fades again, it's just you and me,
Wrapped in the warmth of our own mystery.

[Outro]

So here's to the night and the waves' soft hum,
To the sweetest beach party, more to come.
With golden light, fresh breeze so free,
Behind that tree, it's just you and me.

The Coconut Tree

"The Coconut Tree" is a hymn to the quiet strength of nature, a melodic meditation on Life's trials and triumphs, and a poetic invitation to live with purpose, rootedness, and grace. At first glance, it may seem to describe a humble tree found along tropical shores, but beneath the lyrics lies a profound metaphor for the human spirit and our way of being in the world.

The Symbolism of the Coconut Tree

The coconut tree stands tall and slender, often alone, exposed to the full force of sun, rain, and wind. Yet, it endures. This simple, graceful image becomes a mirror for the soul – *"Through storms and sunshine, we never fall."* Life does not promise us calm weather. Storms are inevitable. The message of the song is not to resist Life's changes but to become like the coconut tree: rooted, adaptable, and fearless.

To bend with the wind and sway with the sea is not weakness; it is wisdom. It is the understanding that rigidity snaps, but flexibility survives. This is the yoga of Life, the practice of embracing change without losing our ground.

Rooted in Love, Wild and Free

Perhaps the most beautiful paradox in the song is this: the tree is both rooted and free. Its freedom comes not from detachment, but from its deep connection to the Earth and its environment. The coconut tree is wild, yes – not lost. It is free, but not aimless. In this duality lies a spiritual teaching: true freedom arises from Love, connection, and purpose.

To be *"rooted in Love, wild and free"* is to embody a way of being that is grounded in care – for self, others, and the Earth – while also allowing the winds of Life to move us without fear.

A Life of Giving

The tree gives everything: *"From water to shade"*, *"feeds the hungry"*, *"providing shelter"*. Nothing is wasted. Every part has a purpose. This speaks to an ethic of generosity that flows naturally from understanding one's place in the web of Life. Just as the tree does not withhold its gifts, we too are invited to offer what we have – our time, our kindness, our talents – not from a place of obligation, but from the joy of being part of the great cycle of giving and receiving.

The tree "knows its purpose, it plays its role". This is not just about productivity – it's about alignment. The coconut tree doesn't strive to be anything other than what it is. This is a radical reminder in a world obsessed with comparison and self-improvement: to simply be what you are is enough.

Resilience Through Grace

The bridge line *"When the winds blow hard, don't break or cry, just bend with grace and reach for the sky"* is a masterclass in spiritual resilience. It calls us to meet adversity with fluid strength. To bend – not out of defeat – but out of an inner knowing that all storms pass. To reach upward – not in ambition, but in openness to light, hope, and transformation.

In describing how *"Every part has a gift, nothing to waste"*, the song honours the sacredness of simplicity. In a culture of excess, the coconut tree stands as a symbol of sufficiency. It gives abundantly not by hoarding, but by existing wholly in its nature.

This is a lesson for us: you are already equipped with what you need to make a difference. You don't need to be more, do more, or have more to be meaningful. Just as the coconut tree does not try to be a mango or a pine, we are each called to be fully, gracefully, and truthfully ourselves.

Conclusion: Under the Tree of Life

The final line, *"Under the coconut tree, we find everything"*, echoes the ancient image of the Tree of Life. It reminds us that healing, wisdom, nourishment, shelter, and joy are all within reach – not in distant dreams, but in the everyday rhythm of Life when we live in harmony with our true nature.

"The Coconut Tree" is thus a living meditation. It is a reggae-rooted mantra for resilience, a gospel of grace, and a soulful ode to the power of rooted simplicity. It asks nothing but reminds us of everything: to bend, to give, to stay rooted in Love, and to let the music of Life move us.

Lyrics

[Chorus]

Like the coconut tree, we stand so tall,
Through storms and sunshine, we never fall.
We bend with the wind, we sway with the sea,
Rooted in Love, wild and free.

[Verse 1]

From the seed in the sand, the journey began,
A little sprout grew under nature's hand.
With roots in the Earth and leaves in the sky,
The coconut tree holds its head up high.

It gives what it has, from water to shade,
Feeds the hungry, so none feel betrayed.
It knows its purpose, it plays its role,
Giving Life to the body, strength to the soul.

[Chorus]

Like the coconut tree, we stand so tall,
Through storms and sunshine, we never fall.
We bend with the wind, we sway with the sea,
Rooted in Love, wild and free.

[Bridge]

Oh, Life is like the coconut tree,
You give what you take, you learn to be free.
When the winds blow hard, don't break or cry,
Just bend with grace and reach for the sky.

[Verse 2]

Every part has a gift, nothing to waste,
The roots hold the ground, the fruit brings taste.
Its trunk is strong, and its fronds spread wide,
Providing shelter where all can abide.

When the dry season comes, it stands its ground,
And when the rains pour, it makes no sound.
Through drought and storm, it shows no fear,
A symbol of Life, year after year.

[Chorus]

Like the coconut tree, we stand so tall,
Through storms and sunshine, we never fall.
We bend with the wind, we sway with the sea,
Rooted in Love, wild and free.

[Outro]

So be like the coconut, stand firm and kind,
Give what you can, leave nothing behind.
For Life's a rhythm, a song to sing,
Under the coconut tree, we find everything.

Amani

In Swahili, the word *amani* means Peace.

This is perhaps the most well-known meaning in the East African context, where the word is spoken in prayers, songs, and greetings. To say *amani* in Swahili is not just to refer to the absence of conflict, but to invoke a state of inner calm, communal harmony, and cosmic balance. In African traditions, Peace is not passive. It is active relational harmony – between human beings, the Earth, the ancestors, and the Divine. To live in amani is to walk in rhythm with all creation.

Originally the word derived from the Arabic root ʾmn (أ م ن) which comes the word ʾamānī (أماني), which means: desires, aspirations, and also security and protection.

In Arabic, *amani* can refer to: the soul's hopes or deepest wishes, *a* state of safety – not just physical, but emotional and spiritual. It also means trustworthiness (*amanah*) – a sacred sense of responsibility and faithfulness. Thus, *amani* in Arabic calls forth both what we long for and what we safeguard. It is Peace as a promise and a covenant.

> *To live in amani is to trust the unfolding*
> *of Life with a faithful heart.*

A Word That Breathes Like Prayer

Across the languages, *amani* is a living principle. It suggests:

A state of serenity beyond surface emotion.

A deep trust in the unfolding mystery of existence.

A sacred alignment between the inner self and the outer world.

It is the quiet flame in the heart of a storm, the stillness beneath the movement, the soul's unwavering gaze toward Peace.

In speaking or hearing *amani*, we awaken something ancient and universal. It's a word that doesn't just mean Peace – it *feels* like Peace. Soft on the tongue, gentle in the breath, *amani* is the music of surrender, the stillness of presence, the dream of all people and all creatures who long to live without fear.

> 🌿 *May we all carry Amani within —*
> *as a hope, a trust, and a way of being.*

The Way and the Place

In the heart of the Eastern Usambara Mountains of Tanzania, Amani it is also the name of a place: a lush, elevated sanctuary nestled among ancient forests, hidden waterfalls, and winding paths. To reach Amani is to embark on a journey that is never straightforward, never easy, and always longer than expected.

The road that leads there twists and turns through dense green. It is steep, rough, and full of surprises. Just when you think you're close, another bend appears – another climb, another surprising view. Time slows down. Distance stretches. And something in you is asked to surrender.

This road is like a mirror of the inner journey. To reach Amani the place, you must travel the symbolic road to *amani* the state of being: serenity, trust, deep Peace. The difficult terrain becomes a metaphor for our inner pilgrimage. For who among us reaches Peace quickly? Who arrives at serenity without passing through the winding roads of struggle, doubt, detours, and delay?

Each curve challenges your patience. Each rough patch demands presence. And yet, as the road narrows and the world becomes quieter, something begins to change. You no longer rush. You begin to listen – to the trees, to your breath, to your own silence. You begin to understand: Peace isn't the destination at the end of the road. It is how you move along it.

The instrumental song *"Amani"* captures this – not in words, but in movement. The rhythms ebb and flow like the road itself. The music doesn't hurry. It expands, retreats, turns inward, then lifts again. It carries you slowly, gently, with pauses that feel like rest beneath tall trees. It invites you to trust the path, even when it seems unclear.

And when you finally arrive – whether to the village in the mountains or a quiet moment in your soul – you realise the long road was not a mistake. It was the way.

> *Amani is not found at the end of the journey.*
> *It is found in every step we take toward it – and in how we take that step.*

To seek Amani is to surrender to the winding mystery of the path, to lean into the curves, to soften into patience, and to listen deeply to what the journey is trying to say.

The Song

In the gentle embrace of the song "Amani", we are invited into a realm where sound transcends words, guiding us through a serene landscape of introspection and tranquillity.

The composition unfolds with a delicate balance, each note a whisper of Peace, each pause a breath of stillness. The melodies intertwine seamlessly, creating a tapestry that soothes the mind and calms the spirit.

As the music flows, it mirrors the rhythm of nature – the ebb and flow of tides, the rustle of leaves in a gentle breeze, the quiet hush of dawn. It beckons us to slow down, to attune ourselves to the subtle harmonies that often go unnoticed in the rush of daily Life.

In this soundscape, we find a sanctuary – a space where the soul can rest, reflect, and rejuvenate. It is a reminder that Peace is not a distant destination but a state of being accessible in each moment of mindful presence.

"Amani" serves as a gentle guide, leading us inward to reconnect with our inner harmony. It encourages us to embrace stillness, to listen deeply, and to find solace in the simple beauty of sound.

In a world choked by literal and metaphorical fumes, the song "I Want Climate Change" bursts onto the scene like a thunderclap of truth – provocative, poetic, rebellious, and radiant with a fiery compassion. At first glance, the title shocks: *Who would want climate change?* And yet, the genius of the song lies in this reversal. It reframes the phrase. The "climate change" it demands is not about melting glaciers, but about melting hearts.

This is not a song about assumed environmental destruction. It is about the emotional weather of humanity – the poisoned atmosphere between people, the storms of identity, the cold fronts of prejudice, the drought of compassion. It is a song that turns the metaphor into a mirror and asks: Why do people talk so much about the Earth's climate? What does the human climate say about us?

> *Change the weather of our hearts and minds*

This is the call. The chorus comes like a chant, like a mantra at a global gathering around a sacred fire. But instead of ancient gods, we are praying to our forgotten humanity. The song makes it clear: the climate that most urgently *needs* to change is the inner one – the emotional, psychological, social, political, and spiritual climate that governs how we relate to each other.

> Jealousy, hatred, violence – physical and mental murder yeah …

This isn't hyperbole – it's diagnosis. It names the silent, invisible weather systems that suffocate the soul: microaggressions, wokeism, tokenism, passive tolerance, judgment disguised as morality.

From Tolerance to Acceptance

In one of the most powerful lines, the song declares:

> The climate of tolerance, it's making me
> sick. Don't just tolerate me – accept me
> quick."

Tolerance, here, is unmasked – not as virtue, but as a polite form of exclusion. To merely tolerate someone is to keep them outside the gate of your heart. True Peace does not come from endurance, but from embrace.

This is a radical critique of the superficial inclusivity that dominates modern discourse – labels, checkboxes, curated diversity, all while the underlying systems remain untouched. This song dares us to go deeper.

If we accept others, we also accept the differences between us. From their, we can either decide to live together or to go in different direction. Sometimes it is better and safer to love from a distance.

Deconstructing Lies and Ideologies

The verses cut through political binaries and cultural clichés:

> The East is bad, the West is good … the
> Earth is round, don't you see the truth?

This is not just anti-racism or anti-imperialism – it is post-division. The song refuses to let us play the usual games of moral superiority. It dismantles the illusion that conflict is only "out there", in governments or armies. No – it's in how we categorize one another, in the "us vs them" baked into our thoughts.

To demand "climate change" here is to demand a new cosmology: one world with different cultures, one humanity with different religions and values, one heartbeat, but many expressions.

Spiritual Fire in Political Garments

Despite its fierce tone and socio-political message, the song is deeply spiritual. It's a sermon in reggae rhythm, a sacred chant of awakening dressed in urban streetwear. It doesn't point to utopia – it points to a shift in consciousness.

> To know who I am, we need a different kind of flame.

This flame is not anger – it is awareness. It burns away false identities, inherited labels, and conditioned divisions, but also forced, false unity. It calls us back to the soul, the light within, the place where all masks fall away.

A Call to Inner and Outer Activism

Perhaps the greatest gift of "I Want Climate Change" is that it does not call for war, but for wisdom. It does not preach conformity, but truth in diversity. It's a protest song that prays. It's a rallying cry that blesses.

> Let's be the wise of acceptance, not the fools of war.
> Peace is the answer, Love opens the door.

This isn't just a line. It's a spiritual compass in a time of ideological hurricanes. It points the way home – not back to comfort, but forward into authentic humanity.

Conclusion: The Inner Climate is Everything

"I Want Climate Change" is not just a clever word-play. It is a revolutionary invitation. A song that asks:

- Can we discover the racism in anti-racism?
- Can we agree to disagree?
- Can we live without dogmas and ideologies?
- Can we progress without leaders?

It teaches that climate change begins in the mirror. And the only solution is Self-Love as action, truth as speech, Peace as practice.

Let this song be not only heard – but lived. Let us be the wind that clears the sky. Let us be the sun that warms the world. Let us be the climate change we long for.

The Lyrics

[Intro: Spoken Prologue]

Climate change?! Climate Change?!

People can't even control the climate between each
other,
Jealousy, hatred, violence – physical and mental
murder, yeah!
We need a change, a change of the climate of our re-
lations,
A new vibration, a higher meditation.

[Chorus]

I want climate change, yeah, climate change – let's do
it!
Change the weather of our hearts and minds, it's time
to renew it.
I want climate change, a shift from hate to Love.
No more cold winds of separation – let the sun shine
above!

[Verse 1]

The climate of tolerance, it's making me sick,
Don't just tolerate me – accept me, quick!
No more boxes, no more labels, no division in this
land,
I am tired of this neo-racism, it's time to take a stand.

[Pre-Chorus]

You say I'm right or left, you say I'm black or white, or
colour,

But I'm a soul, I'm a spirit – can't you see the inner light?
Don't judge me by my pronouns, don't judge me by my name,
To know who I am, we need a different kind of flame.

[Chorus]

I want climate change, yeah, climate change – let's do it!
Change the weather of our hearts and minds, it's time to renew it.
I want climate change, a shift from hate to Love.
No more cold winds of separation – let the sun shine above!

[Verse 2]

The East is bad, the West is good,
The North is rich, the South is poor – misunderstood.
But the Earth is round, don't you see the truth?
It's not about physicals, it's about our hearts.

[Pre-Chorus]

Zombies with no feelings, deciding who shall live or die,
We've lost our humanity – oh, how we lie!
It's getting hotter and hot, emotions boiling high,
Conflicts escalating, war clouds in the sky.

[Chorus]

We need climate change, yeah, climate change – let's do it!
Change the weather of our hearts and minds, it's time

to renew it.
I want climate change, a shift from hate to Love.
No more cold winds of separation – let the sun shine above!

[Bridge]

Denying the obvious, declaring the absurd,
Ignoring Mother Earth's cry, unheard.
It's all about resources, it's all about the gold,
Delusions of control – it's a story we've been told.

[Chant]

We need a change! We need a change!
Hubris and greed, time to rearrange!
We need a change! We need a change!
Delusions and lies, time to break the cage!

[Verse 3]

We are equal, but we are never the same,
Unity in diversity – that's the game.
Let us accept where we belong, and where we differ too,
It's ok, be cool, let's agree to be true.

[Pre-Chorus]

The real diversity is the freedom of thought,
It's human rights and speech – the battles we fought.
I'm sick of just tolerating, let's go beyond,
To the wisdom of acceptance, where we all belong.

[Chorus]

I want climate change, yeah, climate change – let's do
it!
Change the weather of our hearts and minds, it's time
to renew it.
I want climate change, a shift from hate to Love.
No more cold winds of judgement – let the sun shine
above!

[Outro]

Let's be the wise of acceptance, not the fools of war,
Peace is the answer, Love opens the door.
We are one, but we're many, unique like the stars,
Under the same sky, no matter who we are.

Climate change, yeah, climate change – let's do it!
Love and unity – we need to pursue it.
Peace, acceptance – it's time to groove it.
We want climate change, yeah, climate change – let's
prove it!

[Final Outro]

Jah blessings and Love – climate change, let's do it!
One heart, one Love, one world, let's renew it!

Appendix

Further Reading

Mambo Poa - Surfin' the Waves of Life

A Contemplative Songbook

Jay Joyful

Paperback, 104 pages, ISBN 9783769305302
E-Book, ISBN 9783769369984

Dive into the spirit of Peace, Joy, and soulful rhythms with this contemplative songbook inspired by the album Mambo Poa - Surfin' the Waves of Life. This beautifully crafted book invites you on a journey through the ebb and flow of life, celebrating the highs, embracing the lows, and finding harmony in between. Featuring lyrics, reflections, and musical insights for each song, including "Beach Boy Dreams," "Fisherman's Story," and "Love Is Love," this collection is a companion for seekers and dreamers alike. Whether you are singing along, reflecting on the messages within the songs, or simply soaking in the vibrant energy, Mambo Poa will inspire you to ride life's waves with joy, resilience, and gratitude.
Each page flows with creativity, weaving together reggae beats, spiritual insights, and contemplative moments. With its colourful design and soulful content, this songbook is not just a guide but a reminder to live fully - dancing with the tides, surfing every wave, and enjoying the journey.
Catch the rhythm. Ride the wave. Live the joy.

Peace - Real Power Comes from Love, not Hate

A Book About Pacifism, Non-Violence and Civil Disobedience

Jörg Berchem, alias Jay B Joyful

Paperback, 368 pages, ISBN 9783769352887
E-Book, 9783769374971

As you delve into these pages, you'll encounter the diverse tapestry of pacifist thought, from ancient philosophers to modern visionaries. The book serves as a manual for Peace, inviting introspection, dialogue, and action. It inspires a collective awakening to our potential as architects of Peace, urging us to dismantle structures perpetuating violence and fostering a shift in individual and collective consciousness.
This work isn't just a dream; it's an invitation to turn dreams into reality. In a world yearning for Healing and Peace, this book extends a hand, urging us to embark on a shared journey towards a future where Peace isn't just a distant dream but a lived reality.

The Gospel of Love and Peace
Essene Books I to IV
by Edmond Bordeaux Székely

Jörg Berchem (ed.)
Paperback, 420 pages, ISBN 9783741285820
Hardcover, 420 pages, ISBN 9783739241692
E-Book, ISBN 9783741278815

For the first time all translations of the Essene scripts in one volume, revised, newly arranged and edited by Dr. Jörg Berchem. With many illustrations by Caspar David Friedrich, Rembrandt, Leonardo da Vinci and Gustav Doré.

These teachings are unique, because they do not refer to a specific culture, they refer to man and his relationship to his co-beings and his relation to God. They do not demand a specific moral life according to exact rules how to live. They just express a spiritual ethics.

The Teachings of the Essenes
From Enoch to the Dead Sea Scrolls

Jörg Berchem (ed.), Edmond Bordeaux Székely

Paperback, 148 pages, ISBN 9783758300127
E-Book, ISBN 9783758388934

This book gives a deeper insight into the world view and teachings of the Essene Communities as describes in the original texts which have been published in the book "Gospel of Love and Peace".
The author describes and explains the communinions with the Angels as practised by the Essenes.

Meditations of the Children of Light

Communions with the Angels according to the Essene Gospel of Peace

Jörg Berchem

Paperback, 148 pages, ISBN 9783758326561
E-Book, ISBN 9783758333361

In this book, seven morning and seven evening meditations are introduced, which are based in content on the writings of the Essenes, as found in the Essene Gospel of Peace. The author also provides insight into the world-view of the Essenes, their teachings, and spiritual practices.
The meditations establish connections with inner and outer forces, to approach them with greater mindfulness. The practice of these contemplative meditations can lead to healing and inner peace.

The Sevenfold Peace

Contemplations for Universal Peace According to the Essene Gospel of Peace

Jörg Berchem

Paperback, 148 pages, ISBN 9783758329517
E-Book, ISBN 9783758344855

How can one find inner and outer peace in a world without peace?
This book presents seven peace meditations based on the writings of the Essenes, as found in the Essene Gospel of Peace. The author also provides insight into the worldview of the Essenes, their teachings, and spiritual practices.

Divine Moments of Wisdom

Volume 1
100 Contemplations for Spiritual Growth inspired by the Essene Gospel of Peace

Jörg Berchem

Hardcover, 412 pages, ISBN 978-3-819295577-0
E-Book, ISBN 978-3-81923644-0

In a world that often feels loud and hectic, this book is an invitation to pause and reconnect with the quiet wisdom of the soul. Inspired by the Essene Gospel of Peace - an ancient spiritual text filled with Love for nature, divine order, and Inner Peace - this first volume offers one hundred contemplative reflections to accompany you through the rhythms of daily living.
Each reflection is like a gentle light along your inner path - encouraging, healing, and deeply moving. Whether to begin your morning with intention or to wind down in the evening with mindfulness, these words open a space for stillness, awareness, and spiritual growth.
A true treasure for anyone who longs to look deeper, to come closer to themselves, and to rediscover the sacred in everyday Life.
A book for seekers, Lovers, and nature-connected souls - for all who wish to remember what truly matters.

Peace is Possible

Music Album with 14 Songs
Jay Joyful

An Album of Hope, Unity, and Transformation

In a world longing for harmony, "Peace Is Possible" delivers a powerful message through music. This album is a heartfelt journey through the struggles, hopes, and triumphs of peace, reminding us that true change begins within.
With melodies that touch the soul and lyrics that ignite the spirit, "Peace Is Possible" is more than an album — it's a declaration, a movement, a promise. Let this music inspire you to believe in a world where Peace is not just an ideal, but a reality.
Because without Peace, everything is nothing.

www.Joyful-Life.org